forthright

Andrea Boyd

forthright

ISBN: 978-1-7348396-2-3

Cover Graphics by Jeffrey Cohen
Cover Illustration by Sharon Brooke Uy
www.sharonbrookeuy.com

Author Photograph by Erin Adams
www.erinadamsphotography.com

Printed in the United States of America.

First printing edition 2020.

Andrea Boyd
dreboyd@mac.com
www.satoribirths.com

This book is dedicated to all of those along my journey who have opened my eyes to the suffering and beauty around me. To the venerable Ruth Bader Ginsburg. And, of course, to the magical bird of peace that is my son.

PREFACE

These poems are an expression of horror and beauty, dark and light, pain and empathy. Our ability to discern, to consider how others might feel, our ability to face the atrocities honestly, and our willingness to love, will carry us forth into more gentleness and our innate wisdom.

We all have shared consciousness, shared experiences and emotions, shared frustrations and desires, shared air we breathe, vibrations we feel, land we live on, sky we gaze at, oceans we swim in. Everything, everyone, everywhere-gives us clues, lessons, revelations, and insight into our potential as human beings.

Brevity, integrity, and truth are gifts we leave for future generations.

Thank you for reading.

Love,
Andrea
August 2020, Mount Pleasant, SC

CONTENTS

20 Poems For Reflection

20 Poems for Connection

20 POEMS FOR REFLECTION

"Revelation must come before revolution."

-Glennon Doyle, *Untamed*

Revolution

I imagine that the only rules a revolution has
Are those set by nature.
That revolution is naked and doesn't
Have a dress code.
Where "indecent exposure" isn't the blessed
Bodies we've been given.
Indecent exposure is the revealing of what is not
decent, What treatment isn't decent.
And this is the cruelty to innocent creatures
Of which I speak.
The revolution won't have a limit,
Won't be according to a permit.
What permit do we need to be free?
What permit is required that permits one to pay
someone else to kill for a fleeting pleasure on the lips,
feet, back, arm, skin? The permit of human being?
What if we stopped with this word human, and just
said being? Would that help? Or would we still find
our treatment of these others permissible?
I imagine revolution to be off the clock of time,
No 9 to 5. Instead,

By the rhythms of life, the rhythms of rhyme.
It's okay if you don't like it, don't like me, are afraid,
Appalled by what I say, by what I do.
My goal is not to impress you,
But to press upon buttons
That might be the alarm.

It's East-her, Not East-him

They had blood on their hands,
We have blood in our cloth,
The patriarchal knife trying to cut us all off.
Our fire is for burning, the coals need more stoking,
We're not a measly cigarette,
And not here just for smoking.

Limitation to a god, the goddess set aside,
My goodness why like death do we,
Her power try to hide?
Afraid that it will quash you, take away your pride,
Leave you immasculated, taken for a ride.

The womb, it housed us all. Domination makes us fall-
ter. Her and she, writing her-story.
Worship at that altar.

If you destroy, we create, if you hate, we love.
If you stoop below, you'll find us up above.
You hit because your physique,
Your violence makes you weak.

We grow up hearing his, he, him,
And the embedding is done.
Ingrained and rained upon us,
And to you it means you've won.

The womb, it housed us all. Domination makes us fall-
ter. Her and she, writing her-story.
Let's worship at that altar.

Domination of the Feminine: Lactose Intolerant

You've been confined to a room the size of your closet all day long. Standing and eating. Standing and eating. Antibiotics and animal refuse.

You cannot move. You're enslaved. Imprisoned.

A strange male opens the door and shoves a metal sperm gun elbow-deep into your vagina, and fires.

You become pregnant. Your baby arrives, and is stolen from you shortly after birth.

Then, metal clamps are attached to your nipples, and you are hooked up to a milking machine.

Moments later, you are "inseminated" and pregnant once again. Simultaneously with child and lactating.

You're given excessive amounts of hormones to produce 100 pounds of milk per day.

Your baby is gone. There is crying, anguish, stress, sadness, panic, and fear.

This happens over and over again for the next four years.

With your breasts stretched and bruised, ankles swollen, and your heart broken, you are now considered useless—a "downer."

You're thrown in the back of a truck with no food, drink, or light, and headed to confinement once again, this time getting beaten and tortured until it's time to become a "piece of meat," and your skin-a pair of shoes, a belt, or a purse.

This is the plight of a female cow—the sacred feminine. Approximately three and a half million of our sister cows are slaughtered every day.

They are treated as slaves, exploited, raped, and abused, just as human womb-en are today. Their bodies are used as machines, for money, because of their reproductive capabilities. Their children are stolen.

Being a feminist is being tired of gender inequality,

a patriarchal mentality, violence, and disrespect

to those who bring new life into the world.

Being a feminist is having "udder" care for the Divine Feminine—Mother Earth and all of her creatures.

I stopped drinking milk, eating eggs, cheese, and animal flesh, for all of the womb-en, whatever species.

Where Do I Get My Protein?

It's the tired old question, asked time and again,
If you're not eating meat, then
Who, what, where, when
Do you get your protein?

If not from dead cow, or the flesh of a pig,
Or flesh of a carcass, however small or big.
Because protein deficient is not a common issue,
I don't mean to be rude, or try to dismiss you.

But protein is found in so much food,
Nuts, spinach, potatoes, tofu.
Seitan, legumes, tempeh, and beans,
Nutritional yeast and dark leafy greens.
Spirulina, quinoa, grains, and green peas,
Oats, wild rice, sweet potatoes, chia seeds.

Soy milk, soy beans, amaranth too,
Hempseed, spelt, lentil stew.
Broccoli, asparagus, and Brussels sprouts.
Bananas, spinach, and sauerkraut.
Guava, mulberries, blackberries, nectarines,

Potatoes, artichokes, lima beans.
Nut butters, breads, chickpeas, and more,
When the question is asked, they may get bored.

Start listing these treats, they are likely to salivate,
Yes, I can get enough protein on my plate.
Thank you for asking and being concerned,
Was it simply to challenge, so I could get burned?
Let's instead celebrate the efforts being made,
By people who want to stop slaughter and trade,
Who know there's abundance from the ground & trees
Who want animals and people to live a life of ease.

So next time the query is about protein,
You can always ask them, "What do you mean?"
Then ask them where they get vitamin A, D, and C?
And how many grams per day for she or he.
Then you can ask if they've ever stopped to think,
About the amount of pus in the milk that they drink.
Then inquire as to where they get their
Head meat, animal feet, animal skin, blood and liver,
And if eating small intestines and fatty tissues
Ever makes them quiver.

Then suggest they watch a film or two,
And get an education,
So they're more informed about what they consume,
Before the next conversation.

Equal Pay

Why is it, exactly, that men should be paid more,
For the same exact job as a she?
Because she has a vagina instead of a penis,
Or because she's considered to be-
Someone who's supposed to take care of it all,
And receive not much in return?
The martyr, the servant, the wife, a maid,
How we are seen must now be unlearned.
You're threatened by us, so you want to control,
Hurt, belittle, and use.
The days of disrespect continuing onward is
A future we simply refuse.
So if I'm getting paid less because I'm a girl,
And this is how it's always been done,
I think it's time we all say, "We quit."
Until equal pay is won.

Justice For All

Cops killing simply because color of skin.
Guns shot at children and women and men.
Innocent people like Archie are jailed.
Life taken away because the system has failed.

Active shooter drills at schools.
Police who make their own rules.
Strangling, kneeling on necks, while a human being
pleads, "Please, please, I can't breathe. I can't breathe."

Floyd didn't resist-they got it on tape.
Archie's fingerprints weren't found.
At a traffic stop, rundown by a cop and shot,
An unarmed man, named Walter Scott.
Trevon chose a hoodie, Malcolm's evidence destroyed,
Crimes they didn't commit. Just being young boys.

It makes me feel sick, this hurting each other.
The kids are watching us sisters and brothers.
Every incident is a wake up call,
Isn't it liberty and justice for ALL?

Name Calling

The days of calling us bitch, cunt, slut, whores,
skanks, and our vagina as a pussy,
From men who think they're superior,
and were likely once called a wussy.
Should come to an end, with apology too,
it's not only degrading to us, but to you.
You revel in our bodies,
you were birthed by us, did you forget?
An innocent little baby boy- crying, hungry, wet.
A woman brought you forth,
and gave you all she could,
Whether it was what you wanted,
or if you'd call it good.
Somehow you decided, amidst your pubescent day,
that speaking about women like this
was accepted and okay.
Saying you "drilled" "banged" "screwed" or "hit it"
may make you feel you're tough.
But you all just sound like ass holes,
trying to compensate for not feeling enough.
I'm calling out your names today,

to ask you now to cease,
And bring forth a world,
where you respect every girl,
and language is part of the peace.

The Mole Truth and Nothing But

I grew up with a mole on my body, we spent 42 years
together and then I had it cut from my flesh.
I asked for it to be done, it was not against my will,
my wrists and ankles weren't placed in arrest.
After it was gone, I lamented, felt sad,
because it had been a part of me for all the years.
I thought of the men, the newborns and then,
the children being cut and their many tears.
A mole is a growth, but a penis-an organ,
the glans- a functional foreskin that is meant to be.
It's highly sensitive, and belongs to their person,
we call it autonomy.
So my mole is gone and I may miss it some
but my labia is still in tact.
Parents if you want to think circumcision's
YOUR choice,
well I'm sorry,
you're wrong about that.

Circumdecision

Cut your son, you cut yourself.
Who will he come to when he needs help?

Protector of the family, give me a break.
You're sleeping. It's time your consciousness wake.

You cowardly step back and let the pay for hire,
Douse the glans of the masculine fire.

What is the cost to cut your son?
Do you know, do you care, why aren't you the one?

Do it yourself if it means so much,
And let him know that that's your touch.

It's not even your choice. It's cruelty, through and through.
Please tell me mom and dad, how much could WE pay you?

You Disgust Me

I'm sick and appalled,
To hear this horrific new measure.
About perverts luring children
To bring them some pleasure.
Desperate they sit, and ruin a childhood,
Because they've no morals,
And have forgotten their own good.
They cowardly text an innocent girl,
To feel a smidgen of false self-esteem.
One day when she's older if she even survives,
She'll hope it was just a bad dream.
"Text me some pictures," he invites them to do.
Why not look at a Playboy instead?
Stop stealing their innocence, and chop off your penis,
Then maybe you'll think with your heart,
Not your head.

Cut It Out

We've gotta cut the cord, as fast as we possibly can!
So we can take the blood and sell it to the man.
We'll say it's the bilirubin,
We're doing it for their sake.
That's unsubstantiated, not peer reviewed,
So give us all a break.
It's about control—you want to claim it,
And take away her throne.
So you can take the baby too,
And leave it all alone.
To weigh, measure, stamp their feet,
& prick them 'til they bleed.
Come on people, ask yourselves,
What does the baby *really* need?

Vaccines

How many doses can one child take,
It's Russian roulette, you know?
Some body's body can handle them,
But another's might altogether go.
You inject toxins, you get disease,
They're small, they're drugs, come on please.
Listen up sheeple, time to question the herd,
Immunity with mercury, that is simply absurd.

The Hell

A family friend, Amy's older brother, my sister's ex-
Boyfriend, all of these are Chris.
Several years back, my parents sat me down,
And said something like this.
We wanted you to know, before its made public,
That Chris was sexually abused in eighth grade.
He was in therapy for drug use,
When the images resurfaced,
And stood up in a fit of pent-up rage.
It all came flooding back to him, the trips across the
border, the car, the church, his family's living room.
His life after that was a search for escape,
The memories buried down in deep doom.
A priest at our church had repeatedly molested him,
And told Chris it was a secret he must keep.
So he went through school, played sports, excelled,
And never once a word of it did seep.
My mother was solemn, so sad that it happened, the
father of Chris had told her some days before.
I said to my mom, I hope never again,
Will you go to that church anymore.
That priest had been moved,
From another city, you see,

Where he'd been accused of the same sickening deed.
But our school accepted him, and the clergy all knew.
As I recalled them all, the angrier I grew.
I felt betrayed, my childhood a farce,
Their Catholic bullshit a great big sham.
Wearing our uniforms, obeying the rules,
Saying our sirs and mam.
Teaching us about Jesus, God, and the bible,
Requiring we sit in confession and pray.
While raping a young man, and he's not the sole one,
There were others who came forth the very next day.
So, tell me, St. James, are you even remorseful?
You knew this went on, and you turned a blind eye.
My friend's life was ruined, he barely got through it,
I'm not sure Jesus is your guy.
This isn't isolated, thousands have been hurt, and
priests just get transferred? That's swell.
You think people who aren't Catholic,
Get abortions, are gay,
Are the ones who are going to hell?

The Corona Virus

One day in March, we all heard the news,
A virus was spreading around.
It was worldwide and new, no one knew what to do,
The governments ordered to shut all things down.
Some people rejoiced but many were stressed,
No work meant no money or food.
Unemployment was filed, schools closed for a child,
The pandemic, it altered the mood.
No one could go anywhere, see anyone,
Touch anything, until there was data to learn.
In a world where we usually can hug, kiss, and get
close, these suggestions caused tremendous concern.
Keep six feet apart, it's called social distancing,
Stand back and await for your turn.
Still people refused, more people got sick,
More bodies to bury and burn.
In line outside a grocery store, masks covering our
faces, Staffers sanitizing carts.
Once inside the store, with my kid who's now four,
Smiling at others with our eyes and our hearts.
This won't be over until we find a vaccine,
That's the end-all answer they think.

The question is the answer, and should be
the main theme,
Will this corona be the brink?
Eating animals, selling them, caging them, wet
markets, Meat markets, factory farms.
How can we figure to do this to them,
And feel we'll be scot-free of harm?
A vaccine's not the answer, they're harmful too,
Karma is a law, so look at what we do.
Now the people are inside, like animals in cages,
It's time to write a new book to read,
Turn over a new leaf of pages.

Hazing

Oooo here is a great idea,
Try to feel good about yourselves you guys!
By pouring some vodka into a younger boy's eyes.
Or make them get nude in front of a party,
Or deprive them of sleep, cause that'd be so funny.
Hey, what about making them have sex with a goat?
Or drink alcohol until they burn their throat.
Or have them ingest bugs or wet dog food,
Or pour boiling hot water on them,
That'd boost the mood!
Or how about threaten them with
Objects in their anus,
They want to be one of you,
So it's really not that heinous.
Verbal abuse, threats, torture and burning,
How do you do this without your
Conscience discerning?
It's not just the men. It's sororities too.
Emotional humiliation is the big thing for you.
Ladies, you get to choose your pain:
Use a dildo in public or take a hit of cocaine.
To have a boob ranking, they take of their shirts,
Then they might get paddled 'til

They can't sit from the hurt.
Tell me, "pledges," "rushees,"
Why would you even consider this
To feel good about yourself, or try to fit in?
Please let me give you some words of advice,
Anyone who treats you like that,
Is not ever your friend.
And to those of you bullies who are hazing away,
Please try to feel loved, in an entirely different way.

Ammendments 1,2,4,5,9

The **first** amendment prevents the government from
creating or favoring a religion,
but we know that's not the case.
It's all about Christianity, as the president holds
a bible right aside his lying face.

The **second**, and most coveted, "right to bear arms,"
the hunters and mass shooters' delight.
And those who feel safe with a gun in their pocket
or house in the middle of the night.
The gun obsession, false sense of security,
causes more harm than good.
Suicides, children's accidents, or police just firing
because a black kid has on a hood.
Shooting ranges, gun shows,
or a Dicks sporting store,
You can easily get hold of a gun,
if you're twelve, or if you're four.
Isn't it great, this right to have a gun?
Until someone pulls the trigger
and then their life is done.
Regulations denied, NRA paying politician fees,
it's "unconstitutional" to require IDs...

Or background checks, hey! Don't infringe upon me,
How will I go on my killing spree?

The **fourth amendment** bars the government from
unreasonable search and seizure,
yet police consistently stop and frisk.
Racial profiling, cuffing, hitting,
without incurring any risk.

The **fifth** one says people can't be imprisoned without
fair procedures and trials,
it's called due process of law.
But ask Archie Williams who served 40 years,
before being released when they finally saw.

The **ninth** one states that listing specific rights in the
Constitution doesn't mean there aren't
others not spelled out in pen.
Since they were written in 1787 by only men,
it might be time to revamp it then.

Big Pharma

Big Pharma, the world's pharmaceutical industry,
Makes trillions of dollars off you.
There is fraud, scandals, bribery, lawsuits,
But big business, they continue to do.
Johnson and Johnson, Pfizer, Gillead,
GlaxoSmithKline and Merck.
All of their advertising, promotions, and lobbying,
Seem to really work.
60% of Americans take prescription drugs,
And that's why they're so rich.
They contribute 2/3 of the FDA's budget,
Were you aware of this?
That's the U.S. Food and Drug Administration,
Formed to ensure safety and protect the public health.
Interesting that these drug companies
Are supplying most of their wealth.
The FDA approves medical devices,
What Big Pharma also makes.
Is this making sense now,
The corruption, the money, and advantages they take?
Big Pharma uses profits to pay for
Lobbyists on Capitol Hill,
1,400 of them influencing legislation

And guess who's footing the bill?
The founder of the world's largest vaccine maker,
Has a 10 billion dollar net worth,
The population is being drugged,
and it begins right at birth.
Take this for this and that for that,
And this will help reduce the fat,
And if you feel like this from that,
Then take this one to help combat.
It is time for the nations to take control,
Of their body and mind, their health and soul.

For Parents

Adults complain about children "whining,"
But do it all the time,
It's just called complaining instead,
But essentially it's also a whine.
Then read them books, teaching animal sounds,
The oink, the cluck the moo,
Then feed them the dead body parts,
Of those and others too.
I was made to learn the commandments
From the bible at a younger age.
"Thou shalt not kill," and that's the end,
It doesn't say "humans" on a next page.
Being a parent, is a role to fulfill,
Where example is supreme, and takes great skill.
How about consider the child is the wiser?
Who has come to reveal that you might be a miser.
Controlling with threats, bribes, & ice cream,
Spanking, time outs, yell and scream.
Vaccine shots, sugary food and drink,
Never asking them what they think.
Or what they need, or how they feel,
Just spouting orders, making a deal.
Look at them, if they're at the table,

Or standing there listening too,
When talking to other adults, include them,
Just as you would want done to you.
If you're in hurry, know they are not,
They live in the moment you see,
They can't walk as fast, their legs are much shorter,
Slow down for them with glee.
These children are whole, intelligent, fragile,
Innocent, little, pure and sweet,
Look in their eyes.
Who is it you meet?

Birth Like A GD Cheetah

"I'm getting induced in two days," she said.
Why? Was the question I posed.
"Because my doctor told me to."
Why? I wanted to know.
"It's 39 weeks, and the baby's getting big, so she said
That's the best bet."
Why? I said. What about the baby?
Perhaps they aren't ready yet.
"I'm cool with it, I trust my doctor,
They know much more than I do."
Well, I said, do you know of Pitocin- the drug they'll
Inject into you?
"No, never heard of it, I just know to show up
This Monday morning at 5."
Do you want me to tell you,
So you know some about it?
"Nah, I'll get the epidural. Natural-there's
No way I'm gonna try."
Why not just give it a shot? I said.
The sensation is part of the plan.
"Because I'm a wimp, everyone says it's easier,
and I just don't think I can."

Ladies, why the doubt of your strength, resolve,
love, and power?
Stop telling yourself and each other the lies,
That you're still standing in that tower.
Waiting to be rescued by someone else,
Whether doctor, a man, or a drug,
Look in the freaking mirror and smile,
Pat your back, give yourself a hug.
Don't listen to the ones who are afraid,
And share their own fears with you.
Instead, hold your head up high and state,
"There is nothing that I can't do."
Your baby chose you to birth their soul,
It's time you met your lioness,
Believe in your capacity to labor and birth,
The cloth of worry undress.
Walk into the birth like a goddamn cheetah,
You've got everything you need.
Confidence reigning, follow your breath,
Your body, and baby's lead.

The Arrogance of Humans

Such arrogance, to poach wild animals,
And sell the ivory from their tusk,
To steal Rhino horn because you think it cures cancer,
That's ignorance and disgust.
You want the skin of tigers and leopards,
What about we take your skin instead?
How would you feel, if your life we did steal,
To lay your skin on a bed?
Money hungry, you go after them with guns,
Because if not, they'd tear you to pieces,
How to you go to sleep at night,
Knowing your helping to end a species?
And poaching is hunting-just a different word,
So if you're out there hunting, that's also absurd.
You say, oh elephants, rhinos, and tigers I love!
Then go out to shoot turkeys, deer, and dove.
That's the same as saying,
I wouldn't eat my dog or cat-NO!
But, sure, to chickens, cows, fish, turkeys, snails, ox,
rabbit, Baby calf, and on and on I could go…
If you're a poacher,
Find another way to make money please,
There are infinite possibilities.

If you go hunting, get a new frickin' hobby,
There's a lot of other things to do.
How about shoot skeet, or targets instead,
Oh and leave the ducks alone too.
And while I'm on the subject,
Stop running with the bulls in Spain,
Just have the damn fiesta people, you can get drunk
Without causing so much pain.
How about SeaWorld, a prison for orcas,
Where people sit and clap and get sprayed in the face?
Did you know that they rape them,
So they'll have more to confine,
Don't you deem the tiny concrete tanks a disgrace?
What if you lived in only your closet,
And couldn't go anywhere else on Earth?
These freedoms we take,
From these creatures so great,
Are causing us all the most hurt.
I'll end this now, but this could go on,
Enough and more, to fill the book.
Watch the movie called *Earthlings,*
It's time every human took a look.

Screenery

The true religion of the era: profit at all cost.
People controlled by electronic devices,
Becoming more and more lost.
Corporations with no regulations,
What do they want us to see?
What do they want us to buy, to like,
Who do they want us to be?
They want our attention, they want us to click,
Want us addicted, like big pharma wants us sick.
Destructive consequences, like depression and rage,
Suicide, and cutting, at way too young an age.
We are profitable to them, if we're staring at a screen,
Twitter, instagram, facebook, snapchat, tiktok-
All difficult to wean.
Manipulation engines, leading to dystopia,
Corroding humanity, is that their utopia?
Choosing what to feed you, what will you post?
How much could we pay you,
To sell this product the most?
Undermining freedom, democracy and truth,
Toxic for our self-worth, happiness, and youth.
Yes, there are advantages, connection to the globe,
But remember that that connection exists,

Without the screen and strobe.
There must arise a solution to the excessive and
Harmful effects.
Collective will, getting off of the phone,
Embracing the feeling of being alone.
Showing our children there's a great
World around them,
Right where they are, in physical space.
This virtual reality, with filters to normality,
Lends to comparing, despair takes place.
Photographs of children, can be used in any way,
But they see their parents on it and trust them,
So it must be okay.
People at a restaurant, no conversations being had,
Couples never talking, because their phone will
Make them most glad.
It doesn't talk back, just gives you photos and
stimulation,
Even while driving down the road,
we risk annihilation.
To scroll, to see, in reality,
We are spending way too much time doing this.
Picking it up, checking it thrice,
Attention span dwindling, what did you miss?
Wondering who liked what you said or shared,

Who is following you, what's the trend?
Getting notified with a beep or message
every time you have a new friend.
Let's take in our surroundings,
Enjoy our space we're in.
Be examples for the kids because,
We can't do <u>this</u> life ever again.

20 POEMS FOR CONNECTION

"There is a voice that doesn't use words. Listen."

-Rumi

Amidst

Amidst a virus, there's herbs and health,
Amidst the poverty, lies abundance-true wealth.
Amidst the fires, there's the water of tears,
Amidst the hurricanes, lies the absence of fear.
Amidst the violence, there's gentleness and peace.
Amidst the unrest, lies the ability to cease.
Amidst the cruelty, there's compassion of plenty.
Amidst the greed, lies the illusion of money.
Amidst the pain, there's the desire to be free.
Amidst the confusion, lies the truth that you are me.

It Will Pass, Or You Will

This too shall pass, is a well-known phrase,
To bring comfort in times of strife.
At any point, it's all in passing,
How fleeting is this life?
Either it will pass, or you will,
That's what Ram Dass said.
You're already it,
Whether alive or dead.

There Is A Way

We can walk along aimlessly, acting aloof,
                    not knowing what we should do or be
The truth is, you may have a license to drive,
                    but listening is the car's key.
Start up the engine, by going inside,
                    and wait for the driver to politely
decide,
Where will you go next, what maybe can happen,
                    who will you meet and when?
How much is your destiny, how much your steering,
                    and when can we do this again?

Restart

The laundry is piled up, the dishes aren't done,
The toilet needs cleaning,
There's another errand to run.
The groceries are out, the grass needs to be cut,
You can't decide which thing to buy,
The baseboards are dirty, BUT…

You have your health, you have a roof,
You have a beating heart,
If you're feeling overwhelmed,
Take 8 long breaths,
And then,
restart.

The Good News Movement

If you turn on the news, on the TV or phone,
It's usually pretty depressing and grim.
With stories of homicide, natural disasters,
And bickering between him and him.
A wise one once said, "What you think about,
you bring about,"
So Sue and Charmaine decided they would,
Bring more positivity into the world,
By focusing on what is good.
They're on a mission to tip the balance
back in favor of the positive stuff.
Because we all need to hear it, and scc it and feel it,
So the times won't be as tough.

Like the story of the one who bought all the flowers in a flower truck, and asked them to park outside a senior citizen complex, so each person could make their own bouquets.

Or of the person who jumped out of their car, to give an umbrella to a woman waiting on the bus outside in the rain.

Or the Dubai airport staff welcoming refugee passengers from Beirut with white flowers.

Or when a family with a child with autism moved into a village in Cyprus, Greece, the village put up helpful signs for him.

Or when a neighborhood in India turns off the streetlights for over a month, to help a robin lay her eggs and nest in peace.

Or a mother in Mongolia planting over 2 million trees in the past 12 years in honor of her son's dying wish.

Or of the 12-year-old girl who invents a device to attach to car seats to prevent hot car deaths by calling parents, authorities, if it detects a child overheating.

Thank you, Good News Movement, for providing us the stories of kindness and love. Those who think good news "doesn't sell," could probably use a hug.

Options

Remember your options, there are plenty indeed.
Remember in giving, ask, "What do they need?"
Remember your patience, always waiting for you,
Remember in speaking, the 3 questions to run
through.
Is it kind, is it true, is it necessary to say?
Will it make them feel better, or worsen their day?
Would you want it said to you, would it make you feel
good?
If the answer is no, then perhaps not you could.

Karmic Ripple

A tree that's once a seed, stretches to the sky of blue
If outside things can grow that much, why not on the inside too?

No one's exempt, from the karmic law, you see, whatever energy you put out to the world, is returned to you by three...it's tripled.
That's the karmic ripple.

Compassion is the course of happiness, the source of happiness,
Imagine how much we need to give back
The universe gives, nature provides,
Karma is what we think, say, and how we act

The ripple gains momentum in the fabric of time and space,
Comes back with much greater force, and hits you in the face.
The karmic debt paid, but the hardship is great,
The way seeds will ripen, can be quick or they wait.

No one's exempt, from the karmic law, you see, whatever energy you put out to the world, is returned to you by three...it's tripled.
That's the karmic ripple.

The Seven Traits

The inherent traits of passionate presence,
Are seven and are these,
SILENCE, the ability to be quiet as we please.
TENDERNESS, the softness that we share with our soul,
EMBODIMENT, the claiming, acknowledging you're whole.
GENUINENESS, the honesty, we are transparent and true,
DISCERNMENT, knowing what to not, and what to do.
DELIGHT, the celebration, pleasure, joy, and glee,
WONDER, the wow, mysterious, free.

Definitely Positively

There is never a moment that you are unloved.
Brazen that into your mind.
The forces that brought you into your form,
Made you one of a kind.
You are definitely, positively,
Protected, connected, and cherished.
The love that brought you forth to the Earth,
Will never, ever, perish.
It is definitely, positively, true.
There is never a moment that you are unloved.
You didn't forget that, did you?

No One Else Like You

The time of wanting to be anything but yourself,
must come to an end.
If you feel anything but love towards yourself,
please listen dear friend.
The way you are made, your hair, skin, your eyes,
Your buttocks, your breasts, your jawline, thighs.
All of it, including, your mind and your heart,
Are uniquely assigned to you from the start.
So don't compare any more, to another and their fate,
Start loving yourself, before it's too late.
There is no one else like you, never has been
and never will be.
Like each snowflake falling from the sky,
You are specifically and distinctively.

Death of Form

It's like "taking off a tight shoe,"
when the spirit leaves the form,
Like the calm pervading the atmosphere,
after the whirlwind of a storm.
It can be years before death,
when the transitioning does start,
Transforming the bones, the skin, the flesh,
each element plays it's part.
The Earth element going first
the flesh and the bones,
Related to the sense of sound,
the vibration, and the tones.
The water element goes next
linked to taste and bodily fluids
Mucous, blood, bile, pus, semen, saliva,
tears, urine and sweat, the tongue and lips
will be gradually less wet.
Fire element is third, and linked to warmth and sight,
The body will cool, the heat withdrawn,
perception shifts into light.
Air element is last, linked to hearing and touch,
communication, wisdom, and mind.
The breath changes pattern, can be louder or stop
for segments at a time.

The heart stops beating, the body turns cold,
blood starts to settle and pool.
Nowhere to go, nothing to do,
free of meaning, purpose, and rule.
No smell, taste, seeing, hearing or touch,
as the sense fields fade away.
There may be visions, simply let them be,
letting go, to become pure space.
Reverse manifestation, limitless, expansive,
dissolving into a nothingness place.

The Cycles

Existence is cyclical.
Planets, seasons, tides, moods, emotions, waves.
The soil turned to grow again,
and books, we turn the page.
Stars moving, moon phasing,
and sun going up and down.
The uterus sheds again and again,
until menopause comes around.
I look out and see leaves on the trees,
but in weeks they will fall to the floor,
The air will get crisp, the citrus will ripen,
and Autumn is here at the door.
From one moment to next, our bodies in flux,
they will never be always the same.
The ah, oo, mm, birth, life, and death,
and *turiya*-the beyond the beyond name.
Pure awareness, transcendent, immeasurable,
neither effect or cause,
All pervading, changeless, self-luminous-
the miracle gives me pause.

Mycelia

Mycelia, threadlike web, underneath our feet,
Vital to ecosystems, air we breathe, food we eat.

Vegatative fungus, fruiting bodies appear in the ground,
Sometimes in fairy rings, where an arc of mushrooms is found.

Bacterial colonies, helping plant material decompose,
Next time you walk outside on the soil,
know that mycelia is under your toes.

The Nectar of the Breast

The yellow liquid came on que,
A beautiful, glorious, golden hue.
Delivered promptly to me for you.
Colostrum- it's called- and nutrient-dense.
For the baby's first meal, it makes so much sense.
The nectar is sweet, unparalleled and unique,
Every moment, the body adjusts it to meet,
The baby's required nutrients and such,
Your hormones, their skin, your skin, and the touch.
A transference, the substance, the exchange, the trust.
The love, the bond, the two-robust.
This exchange between souls,
While milk flows from the breast,
The baby is soothed, both bodies now rest.

Birthing Anew

The familiar smell of birth begins to fill the room,
It's a variety on earths sweet perfume.
The real blood, sweat, and tears
Coming not from a fight,
But a mother transforming in the middle of the night.

Downstream to the Summit

The ability to see someone's faults, is a low-end talent.
The real talent is to see virtue- a much rarer skill.
With the grace of great beings, and company of truth,
We ascend to the summit, with blessings we fulfill,
Our destiny, evolution, and cosmic consciousness,
The party is always and forever increasing with bliss.
Because everything is eternal, nothing is ever lost.
Turn off the mind, to float downstream,
Those bridges, when you get to them, will be crossed.

Psychedelic

Pysillocybin alters the state of mind and being,
Normal perception through the senses,
Is exposed to another state of seeing.
The walls-they move, the leaves-they speak,
The moon above is in my reach.
She has blue hair, is definitely a lady,
If you call it "man in the moon,"
You certainly are crazy.
A group just passed us, down the dirt path,
Everyone dressed like hippies,
We both saw it, and ever since,
Only know that it was trippy.
The magic mushrooms, caps and stems,
Serotonin and perspective, like hidden gems.
"We're all one," a message and theme,
"Why do we ever worry?" was somewhere between,
The glory and vomit, paranoia, and bliss,
Coming back into reality- well, this.
Transferring from one to another,
Questioning as "the usual" had begun,
Which was real?
That trip? Or this one?

Remember Your Innocence

I marveled one day, at a photo of friends,
Gazing at my newborn child.
Their faces aglow, smiles full of awe,
Their bodies relaxed, looking free and wild.
No one looked worried, jealous, or stressed,
Everyone was radiant, and looking their best.
I loved seeing this, so at ease in their skin,
The innocence they saw was reflected in them.
All of us were once a brand new body and mind,
Arriving here to play, love, and be kind.
Remember your innocence, rejoice that you're here,
Be gentle and soft, like the day you appeared.

Now

Now is now.
And now is now.
And now is now.
And now is now.
And now is now.
And this poem could go on forever.
Eternity is happening now.

Loving Awareness

You are loving awareness.
Are you loving awareness?

ORGANIZATIONS

Some of the proceeds from this book will go to the following organizations that are working to bring healing and transformation.

Circumcision: Intact America, Doctors Opposing Circumcision, and Intaction

Racism: NAACP

Hazing: HazingPrevention.org and StopHazing.org

Priest Molestation: Survivors Network of those Abused by Priests (SNAPNetwork.org)

Child Pornography: Donate to EndSexualExploitation.org, ChildRescueCoalition.org, and the International Centre for Missing & Exploited Children (ICMEC.org)

Animal Rights: Animal Equality, Animal Welfare Institute, and Mercy for Animals

Women's Rights: National Women's Law Center, EqualPayToday.org, FuturesWithoutViolence.org

Reducing Suffering Through Basic Human Goodness: TogetherRising.org

Birthing: Improvingbirth.org, Saving Mothers, Every Mother Counts

Environment: EarthJustice, Environmental Defense Fund, Eden Projects, One Tree Planted

The Sea: The Sea Shepherd Conservation Society

Preventing Wrongful Convictions: The Innocence Network

Parenting: The Natural Child Project

Anti-Poaching: Chengeta Wildlife, Earth League International, Big Life Foundation, Save the Rhino

ABOUT THE AUTHOR

Andrea is a revered teacher of philosophy, body, mind, and spirit for nearly two decades. She has taught all over the world, but home base is the community and center she shares with her spouse in Mount Pleasant, South Carolina.

Andrea has edited and produced several books and produced 7 albums called *The Spoken Word Series*. She wrote, hosted, and co-produced a radio show called "The Depth of Birth," which is now a book, released June 2020.

She writes lyrics for songs, and poems for birthdays. Shel Silverstein's books enhanced her love of rhyming. The poems she recalls writing in childhood were about rainbows and trees.

www.satoribirths.com

CPSIA information can be obtained
at www.ICGtesting.com
Printed in the USA
LVHW042035201020
669312LV00033B/1788